Yellowstone
National Park

John Hamilton

National Parks

VISIT US AT
WWW.ABDOPUB.COM

Editor: Paul Joseph

Graphic Design: John Hamilton

All photos and illustrations by John Hamilton, except United States Library of Congress, p. 10
(Mammoth Hot Springs by William Henry Jackson) and National Park Service, p. 11 (map of
Yellowstone), p. 24 (bison in winter), p. 25 (grizzly and cubs), p. 26 (wolf), p. 29 (forest fire).

Library of Congress Cataloging-in-Publication Data

Hamilton, John, 1959–
     Yellowstone National Park / John Hamilton.
        p. cm. — (National parks)
     Summary: Discusses the history of this national park, its geological features, plant and animal life,
dangers in the park, and efforts to preserve it.
     Includes bibliographical references and index.
     ISBN 1-59197-427-5
     1. Yellowstone National Park—Juvenile literature. [1. Yellowstone National Park. 2. National parks
and reserves.] I. Title. II. National parks (ABDO Publishing Company)

F722.H28 2005
917.87'52—dc21
                                                                    2003041848

Contents

Old Faithful Geyser erupts in Yellowstone National Park

Yellowstone Country

"There it goes!" At the end of a warm summer day in Yellowstone National Park, a crowd of about 200 people gather around Old Faithful, the most famous geyser in the world. Anticipation hovers thick in the air. At first, a plume of steam and water spits and coughs, like a water kettle almost, but not quite, ready to boil over. The earth trembles slightly, then a dull roar is heard. Suddenly a jet of superheated water shoots from the ground. Thousands of gallons of water spew into the air. The crowd breaks out into wild applause. They've come from all over the world, from all walks of life, to see this show, and it does not disappoint.

Old Faithful sends water soaring more than 100 feet (30 m) into the sky, white plumes lit up by a magnificent high-country sunset. After two minutes, the geyser finally settles down, sputtering to a close. The crowd cheers one last time, then slowly disperses. Some witnesses linger, chattering excitedly or merely staring at the wisps of steam still rising from the hole in the ground.

Geysers, hot springs, mountains, canyons, grizzly bears, herds of bison and elk, thundering waterfalls—it's sometimes hard to comprehend all that Yellowstone National Park offers.

Water bubbles in a hot spring at Yellowstone's Upper Geyser Basin, one of the most popular areas in the park.

The Greater Yellowstone Ecosystem is one of the largest temperate zone ecosystems on the planet. It is a land with an incredible diversity of animals, birds, and plants. Our nation's oldest national park—Yellowstone was born in 1872— is at the heart of a 28,000-square-mile (72,520-sq-km) area of federal lands that preserves many wildlife species and the lands in which they live.

The park itself occupies 3,472 square miles (8,987 sq km), bigger than the states of Delaware and Rhode Island combined. Most of Yellowstone occupies the northwest corner of Wyoming, sitting astride the Continental Divide, although small portions extend into neighboring Montana and Idaho. The park is on a high plateau, with mountain chains surrounding it on all sides. As the West was being settled in the 19th century, the area's remote location and rugged terrain made the land unsuitable for cities or large commercial development. Farsighted conservationists convinced lawmakers to set aside the area for future generations.

Today Yellowstone is a paradise for hikers and campers, with almost 1,000 miles (1,609 km) of backcountry trails. It takes years to really get familiar with the park, yet most people breeze through in a day or two while on family vacation. More than 3 million people visit Yellowstone each year, most in the summer months of July and August. Some complain of the overcrowding that plagues the park's most popular sites, like Old Faithful. But even during tourist season, journey a few paces off the beaten path and it seems as if the park is yours alone.

A mountain goat walks in an alpine meadow on the Beartooth Pass, near Yellowstone's northeast entrance.

How Yellowstone Got Its Name

Yellowstone National Park was named after the Yellowstone River, which starts just southeast of the park, then flows through four canyons on its way to meet the Missouri River near Williston, North Dakota. One of these canyons is the spectacular Grand Canyon of the Yellowstone, in the east-central part of the park. Many people believe the river got its name from the colorful walls of this canyon, but historians have another explanation. North of the park, the river has long stretches of yellow-colored sandstone bluffs that soar above its banks near present-day Billings, Montana. The Minnetaree Indians, who lived in the area, called it "Mi tsi a-da-zi," which means "Rock Yellow River." French fur trappers translated this to "Yellow Rock," or "Yellow Stone." The Minnetaree probably didn't even know about the area we know today as Yellowstone National Park.

Morning light on the Grand Canyon of the Yellowstone.

"Now I know what it is to sit enthroned amid the clouds of sunset." Author Rudyard

Kipling, after visiting the Grand Canyon of the Yellowstone.

The First National Park

In 1806, mountain man John Colter, a former member of the Lewis & Clark expedition, wandered into the area we know today as Yellowstone National Park. He was amazed, not only by the abundance of wildlife, but especially by the steaming hot springs and spouting geysers. After Colter returned to civilization, few people believed his wild tales.

In time other fur trappers, including Jim Bridger and Osborne Russell, began telling of the wonders of Yellowstone. People thought the men were lying when they described the area's thermal features.

By the 1870s, Yellowstone was one of the last unexplored areas in the country. Western settlers had passed by because the region was too rugged. Although Native Americans visited the area more than 11,000 years ago, only one tribe, Shoshone Indians who called themselves the Sheepeaters, took up permanent residence in Yellowstone. Eventually, organized government expeditions explored the area.

Mammoth Hot Springs
photographed by William Henry Jackson in 1871.

"… and behold! The whole country beyond was smoking with vapor from boiling springs; and burning with gases issuing from small craters, each of which was emitting a sharp, whistling sound."
Joe Meek, fur trapper, 1829

10

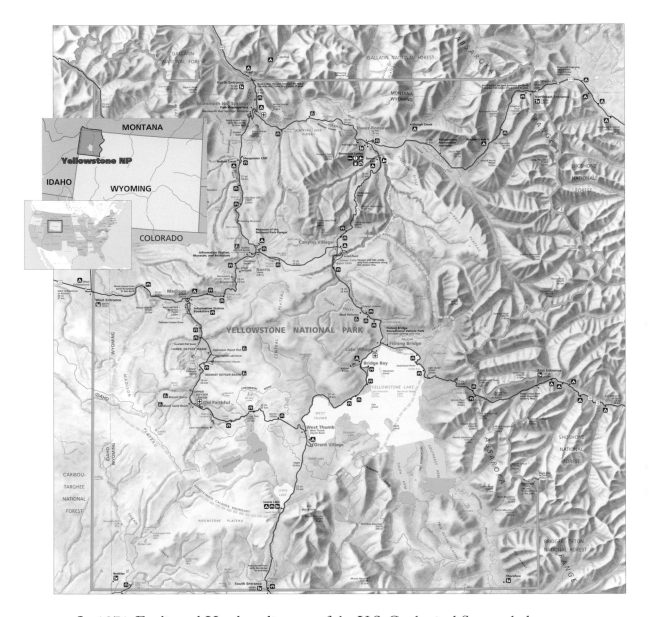

In 1871, Ferdinand Hayden, director of the U.S. Geological Survey, led an expedition into Yellowstone. Two other expeditions had preceded this one, but Hayden had two secret weapons: painter Thomas Moran and photographer William Henry Jackson. These artists brought back visual proof of Yellowstone's wonders.

The Hayden expedition's work had a great influence on the U.S. government. On March 1, 1872, President Grant signed a bill into law setting aside 2.2 million acres (.89 million hectares), making Yellowstone the world's first national park. This preserved the area in its natural state so that new generations could enjoy its beauty for years to come.

The Geology of Yellowstone

Old Faithful is just one of over 300 geysers in Yellowstone National Park. Geysers and hot springs are among the reasons the park is so popular today. Yellowstone has the greatest concentration of thermal features anywhere in the world. New Zealand and Iceland have many geysers and hot springs, but only Yellowstone has so many in one place.

Yellowstone sits atop a geological "hot spot," an area where hot magma deep underground bubbles close to the earth's crust. A gigantic magma chamber, a sea of molten rock just a few miles below the surface, powers the park's more than 10,000 thermal features.

The Yellowstone region witnessed three major volcanic eruptions in the distant past. The first two happened 2 million and 1.3 million years ago. The most recent occurred 640,000 years ago. These eruptions were so powerful that some geologists call Yellowstone a "super-volcano." The latest eruption spewed over 240 cubic miles (1,000 cubic km) of debris across the continent. Lava flowed for thousands of years, and thick layers of rhyolite ash were spread over the region. By comparison, the 1980 eruption of Mount St. Helens resulted in debris one ten-thousandth the amount of Yellowstone's cataclysm.

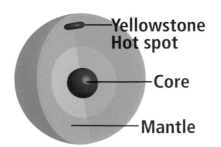

This cutaway view of Earth shows the Yellowstone hot spot just beneath the planet's crust.

The river channel of the Grand Canyon of the Yellowstone exposes rhyolite lava that flowed over this part of the park 480,000 years ago (above). Most of the canyon lies within the boundaries of the Yellowstone caldera. Farther north, at the Golden Gate area (below), the rocks are from an earlier eruption almost two million years ago. The color of the rocks, called "Huckleberry Ridge ash flow tuff," and the yellowish lichen that grows on them, gives the area its name.

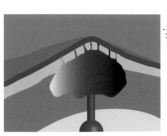

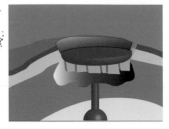

Yellowstone hotspot   *Eruption*   *Caldera forms*

After the eruption, a giant, smoldering crater was left in the center portion of the park. This deep crater, called a caldera, which in Spanish means "caldron," is an oval measuring 30 miles (48 km) wide by 45 miles (72 km) long.

Melissa Young is a park ranger stationed at Yellowstone's Norris Geyser Basin area. "Think of it this way," she explains to people taking her guided tour, "Yellowstone was like a big apple pie that was put in the oven too long. Then someone stuck a fork in the middle of the pie and all the contents exploded outward through the hole. When the eruption was over, the crust fell back to the bottom of the pan." After several thousand years, she explained, the caldera eventually filled with lava.

Nature is constantly changing the Yellowstone region. Thick forests of lodgepole pines have risen from the ashes of the volcano. Glaciers have scoured the land and carved out immense valleys. Hundreds of earthquakes are recorded yearly in the park, most small and unnoticed, some big enough to feel. On August 17, 1959, a large earthquake just outside the park sent an entire mountainside sliding down, killing 28 campers in the landside.

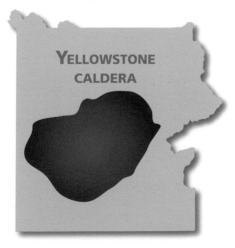

YELLOWSTONE CALDERA

Yellowstone is still the center of intense volcanic activity, and most geologists expect another eruption. Exactly when, they can't say, but probably not in our lifetime. Ranger Young puts it in perspective: "Yellowstone is due to erupt," she says with a smile, "but I don't think it's going to happen during this tour, so let's not worry about it."

A view from **Artist Point** looking into the Grand Canyon of the Yellowstone.

Hydrothermal Wonders

Geyser gazers are people who make a sport of witnessing as many geyser eruptions as they can. Nowhere else in the world is geyser gazing better than in Yellowstone National Park. The majority of Yellowstone's geysers are clustered in flat depressions of land called basins, which are situated mainly in the south and western parts of the park, inside the caldera boundary. The most famous geyser basins include Norris Geyser Basin, Midway Geyser Basin, Upper Geyser Basin, and West Thumb Geyser Basin on the southwest shore of Yellowstone Lake.

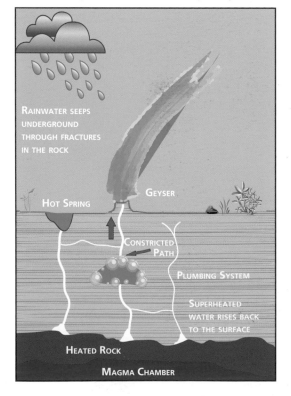

Geysers and hot springs begin when rain and snowmelt seeps underground and is heated up. In Yellowstone, a magma chamber is only three miles (4.8 km) down, which is why the park has so many thermal features. Water sinks to a depth of about 10,000 feet (3,048 m), where it meets layers of rock heated by the magma chamber below. The water is superheated, often to temperatures over 400 degrees F (204 degrees C). The water remains in a liquid state because of the tremendous pressure of the rocks above.

In a **Hot Spring,** the most common hydrothermal feature in Yellowstone, superheated water rises and collects in a pool on the surface. Layers of porous rock act like a sort of complex plumbing system. The water continuously circulates as it cools, sinks, heats up and then rises back to the surface. Brilliant colors are the result of algae, and by the absorption of light by the mineral-laden water. Water on the surface of a hot spring often exceeds the boiling point, which is 199 degrees F (94 degrees C) at Yellowstone's high mountain elevation. Hot springs, like Morning Glory Pool (above) can be dangerous, but are beautiful when viewed from a safe distance. The Upper Geyser Basin (below) contains many hot springs.

• Geysers

Geysers are like hot springs, but they have a constriction in their underground plumbing system, usually close to the surface. Pressure builds up, then is released in a violent eruption of steam and hot water. Some geysers erupt every few minutes, while others wait for years before putting on a show. The most famous geyser is Old Faithful, which is just one in a series of spectacular features in the Upper Geyser Basin. Old Faithful gets its name from the predictability of its eruptions, which occur on average about every 92 minutes. The largest geyser in the world is Steamboat Geyser, in the Norris Geyser Basin. This monster has rare eruptions that soar to heights of up to 400 feet (122 m), almost four times as high as Old Faithful.

• Mud Pots

Mud pots are a kind of hot spring. They are formed when a limited volume of water mixes with clay and other undissolved minerals. This mixture, together with hydrogen sulfide gas, produces sulfuric acid, which dissolves the surrounding rock

into a colorful stew of boiling mud pits. The hydrogen sulfide gas gives the mud pots their distinctive "rotten egg" smell. Mud pots can be very colorful, which is why they're often called paint pots. The most famous in Yellowstone are Artist and Fountain paint pots, and Mud Volcano.

Fumaroles, like this one at Norris Geyser Basin (above), are also called steam vents. They occur when a hot spring has so little water that it boils away before it can reach the surface. The ground trembles and a loud hissing can be heard as a plume of white steam is released into the air.

Canyon Country

The Grand Canyon of the Yellowstone is a 20-mile (32-km) long gash in the earth, formed by lava flows, glacial blockages, and especially the never-ending action of erosion. The Yellowstone River cuts a path through the canyon that is 1,200 feet (360 m) at its deepest point. Exposed along the canyon walls are soft, rhyolite lavas in a riot of colors ranging from reds to deep yellows.

The canyon is one of the most popular spots in the park. Hiking trails hug both rims. Standing at Artist Point along the south rim, tourists take in the breathtaking view of the Lower Falls of the Yellowstone. Dropping 308 feet (93 m) into the canyon, the waterfall is almost twice as high as Niagara Falls. Over 37,000 gallons (140,060 liters) of water roar over its brink each second.

Just upstream are the Upper Falls. At 109 feet (33 m), they are not as tall as Lower Falls, but are still awe-inspiring. The afternoon sun often lights up water spray from the falls, creating crowd-pleasing rainbows.

"… as I took in the scene, I realized my own littleness, my helplessness, my dread exposure to destruction, my inability to cope with or even comprehend the mighty architecture of nature…" Nathaniel P. Langford, 1870, first superintendent of Yellowstone National Park

Lower Falls of the Yellowstone River.

The calcium carbonate of Mammoth Hot Springs (above) creates a spectacular series of terraces. The Lamar Valley (below) is one of many places to spot bison. The valley is winter range for bison and elk. Predators such as wolves and bears also roam here.

Water tumbles 132 feet (40 m) at Tower Fall (above), which is named for the volcanic pinnacles next to the falls. A fisherman (below) tries his luck in the Firehole River. Native cutthroat trout swim in Yellowstone's crystal clear lakes and rivers.

Lake Country

Yellowstone Lake, in the southeastern part of Yellowstone, is the largest North American mountain lake above 7,000 feet (2,134 m). Cutthroat trout and whitefish course through its blue waters, which run more than 400 feet (122 m) deep. The jagged peaks of the Absaroka Range wrap themselves around the eastern shore of the lake.

Yellowstone Lake has over 141 miles (227 km) of shoreline. Visitors have plenty of opportunities for boating and fishing, as well as wildlife viewing and hiking. Bison and moose are often seen in the area. The western part of the lake, called West Thumb, has an active geyser basin.

North of the lake, the Yellowstone River winds its way through Hayden Valley, one of the park's premier places to view wildlife. The valley is the remnant of an ancient lake caused by a glacier blocking the river. Today it is a long, sagebrush-covered valley surrounded by forests of lodgepole pines.

The Yellowstone ecosystem has the greatest wealth of wildlife outside Alaska. In Hayden Valley you can almost always spot herds of bison, or moose browsing in the river. The area is also home to grizzly and black bears. Bears used to be a common sight in the park. Garbage dumps have since been cleaned up, and problem bears aggressively relocated to back-country areas, so that bears are now less often spotted.

A herd of bison roams through Yellowstone's Hayden Valley in winter.

Sunrise over **Yellowstone Lake.** The Absaroka Range rises up in the distance. Yellowstone Lake is the biggest mountain lake in North America.

A grizzly bear and her three cubs.

"There is a majestic harmony in the whole." Nathaniel P. Langford, 1870, *The Discovery of Yellowstone Park*

The Northern Range

The spectacular Beartooth Highway gives visitors an adrenaline-filled high-altitude rush as they enter the northeast corner of Yellowstone National Park. After a drop in elevation of several thousand feet, the road enters the Lamar Valley. It is drier and warmer in this part of the park, with forests giving way to grasses and sagebrush. Elk and bison migrate here to escape the harsh winter weather of the higher elevations. Other animals common to the area include bears, pronghorn, elk, foxes, coyotes, and mule deer.

On a mountaintop south of the road sits Specimen Ridge, which contains the largest petrified forest in the world. More than 100 species of fossilized plants can be found here.

Yellowstone boasts one of the most famous wolf recovery projects in the United States. In 1995, 51 years after the last wolf was killed in the park, 14 wolves were released into the Yellowstone area, transplanted from their home in Alberta, Canada. The pack thrived, and more wolves were later released. Today, there are over 300 of these important predators in the Yellowstone ecosystem. It is a rare ecological success story.

During the last several years, wolf sightings have become more common in the Lamar Valley. At dawn or dusk it is often possible to see them roaming the distant hills, or hear their eerie howl. It is a sound most visitors will never forget, a reminder of wild places undisturbed by humans.

Moonrise over Lamar Valley (above). The Beartooth Highway runs through the Absaroka–Beartooth Wilderness in the distance. Lamar Valley is home to many animal species, including elk (below) and wolves (opposite, top).

Future Challenges

Fire is a natural part of any forest. Unfortunately, for many years the U.S. Forest Service put out every fire it could in the national parks. This created a situation where the forest floor of Yellowstone accumulated layers of deadwood and pine needles, ready to go up in flames.

During the long, hot summer of 1988, drought made the forest tinder dry. The stage was set for disaster. Thirteen major fires, most caused by lightning, swept through the park and burned an estimated 988,925 acres (400,204 hectares) of wilderness.

Many people believed that the entire park had burned to a cinder that summer. But as tourists soon discovered, this was not so. New plants sprouted up almost immediately. The black scorch of groundfires was quickly covered by new grasses and wildflowers. Burned out logs, called snags, soon bleached white and blended with the surviving foliage. Millions of pine trees stand today in the cinders of the old forest. Yellowstone was far from destroyed. The thermal features, the Grand Canyon of the Yellowstone, the magnificent wildlife, all are still there. The landscape has changed, but a new Yellowstone has risen from the ashes.

Fire could not destroy Yellowstone, but other forces threaten its pristine beauty every day. Crowds of visitors, although well-meaning, disrupt the wilderness setting. Commercial development just outside Yellowstone threatens the large animals that migrate beyond the park boundaries. There is also concern that some developments might affect the thermal features that make Yellowstone so famous.

If we wish to protect the Yellowstone we know today, it is crucial that the public and the government work together to preserve this fragile ecosystem, this gift for all future generations.

Fires that swept through Yellowstone in 1988 (above) created conditions for new forest growth (left). More challenging concerns include nearby commercial development and overcrowding (below and opposite top), which threaten the park's natural beauty and ecological balance.

Glossary

CALDERA

A caldera is a wide, craterlike basin that is formed by the explosion of a volcano, or by the collapse of a volcano's cone.

CONTINENTAL DIVIDE

A ridge of the Rocky Mountains in North America. Water flowing east of the divide eventually goes to the Atlantic Ocean. Water flowing west goes to the Pacific Ocean.

ECOSYSTEM

A biological community of animals, plants, and bacteria, all of whom live together in the same physical or chemical environment.

FEDERAL LANDS

Much of America's land, especially in the western part of the country, is maintained by the United States federal government. These are public lands owned by all U.S. citizens. There are many kinds of federal lands. National parks, like Yellowstone, are federal lands that are set aside so that they can be preserved. Other federal lands, such as national forests or national grasslands, are used in many different ways, including logging, ranching, and mining. Much of the land surrounding Yellowstone is maintained by the government, including several national forests and wildlife refuges.

FOREST SERVICE

The United States Department of Agriculture (USDA) Forest Service was started in 1905 to manage public lands in national forests and grasslands. The Forest Service today oversees an area of 191 million acres (77.3 million hectares), which is an amount of land about the same size of Texas. In addition to protecting and managing America's public lands, the Forest Service also conducts forestry research and helps many state government and private forestry programs.

GEOLOGICAL SURVEY

The United States Geological Survey was created in 1879. It is an independent science agency that is part of the Department of the Interior. It researches and collects facts about the land of the United States, giving us a better understanding of our natural resources.

GLACIER

A glacier is often called a river of ice. It is made of thick sheets of ice and snow. Glaciers slowly move downhill, scouring and smoothing the landscape.

MOUNTAIN MAN

An early explorer who lived in the largely unexplored mountainous areas of the American and Canadian west. Many mountain men earned a living by fur trapping.

PETRIFIED WOOD

Ancient wood that has had its cells replaced with mineral deposits. Stony chunks of petrified wood, millions of years old, are common in certain areas of Yellowstone.

PLATEAU

A large, level area of elevated landscape. Yellowstone National Park is a high plateau surrounded by mountains all around.

TEMPERATE ZONE

A moderate climate zone that is found between the tropics and the polar circles.

A petrified tree stump found in Yellowstone National Park.

Index